Daily Problems
and
Weekly Puzzlers
Science

grade
5

by Eleanor Bluestein

ideal

Daily Problems & Weekly Puzzlers
Science

GRADE 5

Eleanor Bluestein taught science for six years in the public school systems of Uniondale, New York, and Potomac, Maryland. She has taught writing at San Diego Community Schools and has worked with beginning readers for Literacy Volunteers of America in San Diego, California. As an independent contractor and as an employee of Harcourt Brace Jovanovich and Curriculum Concepts, Eleanor has written and edited over 20 books, articles, and teacher materials in the field of science.

Eleanor holds a bachelor of science degree from Tufts University in Massachusetts, a masters of education degree from San Diego State University, and a professional certificate in teaching English as a second language from the University of California, San Diego. She has also done extensive graduate work in science education at Hunter College in New York and at the University of Maryland.

ACKNOWLEDGMENTS

Special thanks to teachers Leah and Michael Cole of Diegueño Country School in Rancho Santa Fe, California; Carol McKay and Glenna Yavorsky of Harbor View Elementary School in San Diego, California; and Sylvia Ruvalcaba of Bayview Child Development Center in San Diego, California, for their careful review and student testing of the materials in this book.

Cover Design: Joan K. Takenaka

Cover Illustrations: Ken Bowser

Text Illustrations: Roberta Collier-Morales

Production: Linda Price

Proofreader: Rachel Oberlander

Project Managers: Fran Lesser and Linda Wood

Developed for Ideal by The Woods Publishing Group, Inc.

Art Director: Nancy Tseng

Table of Contents

▼▼▼▼▼▼▼▼▼▼▼▼▼

Introduction

▼▼▼▼▼▼▼▼▼

This book is one in a series of four books for Grades 3 through 6. These books provide a treasury of challenging and engaging problems from all areas of the science curriculum. The Daily Problems and Weekly Puzzlers are each keyed to the appropriate National Science Education (NSE) Standards, and many of them are designed for "hands-on" experiences using common classroom materials.

Students entering the workforce in the twenty-first century will need to have had substantial practice thinking and processing information in different ways. Applying the scientific process in different situations helps students develop useful strategies, techniques, and problem-solving methods that can be used in other areas.

Each book contains 144 Daily Problems and 36 Weekly Puzzlers. The Daily Problems are presented four per page, and most are designed to take 15 minutes or less to solve. The Weekly Puzzlers are more complex, designed to engage students over a longer period of time and to help them develop a variety of science skills. Some Weekly Puzzlers include tips for expanding the activity into a science fair project. Sample answers are provided for the problems, many of which are open-ended or have more than one possible solution.

Suggestions for Classroom Use

The problems and puzzlers are written for Grade 5, but because the ability levels of students vary greatly, you may want to modify the problems to meet your students' individual needs. For example, you could have your "struggling" students solve portions of whole problems or work with partners. You might require your advanced students to provide more detailed explanations, or to extend the problems and puzzlers in other ways. The emphasis, however, should be on having students come up with creative ideas for solving the problems. The process a student goes through in solving a problem is often more valuable to the student's learning than the actual answer itself.

One NSE Standard and one general subject area are referenced for each of the 144 Daily Problems and 36 Weekly Puzzlers. The chart on page vi indicates which problems and puzzlers are related to each NSE Standard. You can refer to the Standards and subject areas to help you decide how to use the problems and puzzlers. You may want to focus on one Standard or subject area for a week or a month; or you may want to expose students to a variety of Standards and areas over a set period of time. Since many of the problems are related to more than one Standard or subject area, you can use the cross-reference chart as a starting point for choosing the problems and puzzlers you want.

The problems and puzzlers may be given to individual students, pairs of students, or small groups. Working with partners or in small groups gives students an opportunity to share their thinking verbally. Often students are better able to express their thinking in writing after they've had opportunities to express them out loud. Talking about problems with others helps students articulate, clarify, and modify their ideas.

Many of the Weekly Puzzlers and some of the Daily Problems ask students to extend the ideas by applying concepts to new situations and by creating their own problems. When students have the opportunity to apply concepts and create their own problems, they understand ideas more deeply and personally. When they are involved in this way, they are constructing their own meaning as they undertake this creative process.

Materials

Many of the problems call for the use of materials. We have tried to choose materials commonly found in the classroom or at home. Some of the problems call for basic science equipment, such as magnifying lenses, thermometers, and magnets.

Hints for Using Problems and Puzzlers

- Use as an early morning warm-up. Put one or more problems on the overhead projector or chalkboard to start your day. Have volunteers explain their answers.

- Give students a Daily Problem or Weekly Puzzler as a daily or weekly homework assignment.

- Have teams work on the same problem during a science-lab period. Then have students take turns explaining answers to the class. Or have groups work on different problems, then rotate the problems when students finish.

- Have an "explanation contest" by seeing who (or which group) can best produce a clear and detailed written explanation of a problem or puzzler with no time limit.

- Use as a transformational activity. Have students turn Daily Problems into Weekly Puzzlers, and Weekly Puzzlers into long-term investigations and explorations.

- Challenge students to create their own problems similar to one or a group of Daily Problems you choose. Compile sets of student-created problems into a quiz for everyone to do. Then correct the quiz as a class so that students can read, answer, and explain their own problems.

- Have students select sample Daily Problems and/or Weekly Puzzlers to put in their portfolios and write about why they chose these problems.

Getting Started

Work through a few daily and weekly problems with your class before having students work individually or in groups. Encourage students to use their critical thinking, reasoning, and science process skills.

Model both effective and ineffective use of skills when working with your class as a whole. Also model exemplary and incomplete written explanations, as well as productive and unproductive communication in groups. In this way, you will demonstrate and clarify your expectations for students when they are using science skills to solve problems in individual or collective situations.

Show students how to help each other. Emphasize that giving answers to a partner does not help either student understand the concepts involved. You can make a game out of this by having students role-play appropriate and inappropriate ways of interacting with a partner or with a group.

Wrapping Up

Involve students by discussing the problems as a class after students complete them. Having students share the methods and strategies they use allows all students to develop new skills. During discussions, it is important to emphasize that many problems in science (and life) have multiple solutions. When students see a variety of answers to a problem and hear how other students reached different conclusions, they are more likely to remain open to more than one path or solution.

Internet Links

The world of science awaits you and your students on the World Wide Web. Listed below are some web sites that may prove useful in the classroom and at home.

The Internet Public Library
www.ipl.org

National Science Teachers Association
www.nsta.org

National Science Foundation
www.nsf.gov

NASA
www.nasa.gov

San Francisco Exploratorium
www.exploratorium.edu

San Diego Zoo
www.sandiegozoo.org

Eisenhower National Clearinghouse for Mathematics and Science Education
www.enc.org

Cross-Reference Charts

NSE Standard	Daily Problem Number	Weekly Puzzler Number
Scientific Processes	1, 9, 17, 25, 33, 41, 49, 57, 65, 73, 81, 89, 97, 105, 113, 121, 129, 137	1, 9, 11, 17, 26
Scientific Thought	2, 10, 18, 26, 34, 42, 50, 58, 66, 74, 82, 90, 98, 106, 114, 122, 130, 138	2, 10, 18, 23
Life Science	3, 11, 19, 27, 35, 43, 51, 59, 67, 75, 83, 91, 99, 107, 115, 123, 131, 139	3, 19, 27, 30, 35
Physical Science	4, 12, 20, 28, 36, 44, 52, 60, 68, 76, 84, 92, 100, 108, 116, 124, 132, 140	4, 14, 28, 36
Earth and Space Science	5, 13, 21, 29, 37, 45, 53, 61, 69, 77, 85, 93, 101, 109, 117, 125, 133, 141	7, 13, 21, 29, 34
Human and Social Science	6, 14, 22, 30, 38, 46, 54, 62, 70, 78, 86, 94, 102, 110, 118, 126, 134, 142	6, 12, 20, 22, 33
Science and Technology	7, 15, 23, 31, 39, 47, 55, 63, 71, 79, 87, 95, 103, 111, 119, 127, 135, 143	5, 15, 25, 31
History and Nature of Science	8, 16, 24, 32, 40, 48, 56, 64, 72, 80, 88, 96, 104, 112, 120, 128, 136, 144	8, 16, 24, 32

Daily Problems

1 Trash Pollution

Hook a rubber band over your thumb. Stretch the rubber band across the back of your hand and hook the other end over your little finger. Try to get the rubber band off without touching anything or using your other hand. What can happen to birds and sea animals when humans pollute beaches with plastic trash, such as rings from six-packs of soda?

Science Superstar: Find out how long it takes for plastic garbage to decompose.

2 Properties of Metals

Have you ever struggled to open a jar with a metal lid? Some people hold the metal lid under hot tap water. Why does this make it easier to open the jar?

Science Superstar: What are some other ways to make it easier to open the jar?

3 Classification

Patti and her family are having a picnic in their backyard. Unfortunately, some uninvited guests are trying to share their dinner. Patti's dad lights a special candle (called a citronella candle) that keeps insects away. Which of the animals listed below would the candle keep away? Which animals might still bother Patti and her family?

| cat | bee | snail | ant | worm |
| fly | wasp | mosquito | blue jay | beetle |

4 Work

Hold a rubber band against your lips. Can you feel how cool it is? Now quickly stretch out the rubber band while holding it lightly against your lips. What do you notice? Why do you think this happens?

Daily Problems

5 The Solar System

Have you ever wondered if humans could live on other planets? Think of at least one problem people would have if they tried to live on Mercury, Venus, or Mars. Look at the diagram for clues.

Science Superstar: How does a planet's distance from the Sun affect its surface temperature?

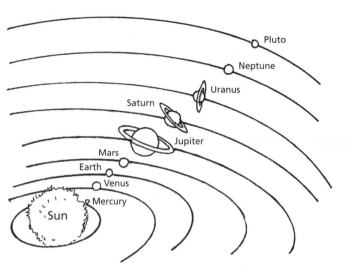

6 Population

Did you know that the number of people in the United States grows by about 2.4 million every year? If there were 248 million people in the United States in 1990, what will the population be in 2020?

Science Superstar: Do you think there are too many people where you live, or is the number just right? If you are still living where you live now in the year 2020, how do you think the increased population will affect you?

7 Inventions

The first cameras were the size of small rooms. Early radios were as big as microwave ovens. The first computers had to be housed in large rooms. Picture these items today. Write a sentence that tells one trend in the technology of modern inventions. How has this trend benefited you? What items do you have that are examples of this trend?

8 Gravity

If you dropped a baseball and a light rubber ball from the edge of a table at the same time, which one do you think would land first? Try it and see! Are you surprised at what happens? A famous scientist named Galileo once asked the same question. What do you think he found out?

Daily Problems

9   Classification

In 1997, a baby whale arrived at Sea World in San Diego. J.J. was only three days old when it was found on the beach. J.J. had been separated from its mother and was very sick. The people at Sea World took care of it. What do you think they fed it when it was a baby? Explain your reasoning.

10   Evidence

Suppose you are walking along a stream and you come upon a scene like the one below. What animal would you think has lived here? What evidence do you see of this? How could you find out if the animal still lives here?

11   Adaptations

You find an injured bird in your yard. You decide to put food near it until it is healthy enough to find food for itself. If the bird has a beak like the one in the picture, what kind of food would you give it? Why? If you didn't know what to feed it, how could you find out?

12   Light

Stare at a small square of red paper while counting slowly to 45. Now stare at a sheet of white paper. What do you see? Repeat the activity with green, blue, and yellow squares. What do you see?

Science Superstar: Why do you think these images occur?

Daily Problems

13 Ecosystems
Earth and Space Science

Look at the picture below. What kind of habitat is this? How do you know?
What three animals might be hiding somewhere in the scene?

14 Food Chains
Human and Social Science

Think of one animal protein you ate today. (Examples: cheese, milk, eggs, beef,
chicken, fish) Then draw a food chain that includes you and the animal the
protein came from. Label each item in the food chain a *consumer* or a *producer.*

15 Safety
Science and Technology

Did you know that companies often test their products before they sell them?
For example, there's a mechanical walking machine that tests shoes to find
out how long they will last. Design a device that could test a car window for
breakage when hit by a rock. Describe your device in words or with a picture.

16 Diseases
History and Nature of Science

In 1945, Sir Alexander Fleming won the Nobel Prize
in Medicine for his discovery of penicillin, the first
antibiotic. Suppose you were presenting the award.
Write the paragraph you'd read to the audience
to explain why the committee chose Fleming for
the award.

Daily Problems

17   Experiments
Scientific Processes

If you did an experiment, what information would you write down so someone else could repeat what you did? Why do you think it's important for scientists to repeat one another's experiments?

18   Galaxies
Scientific Thought

Have you ever looked up at the night sky and seen the Milky Way Galaxy? Astronomers believe that galaxies are like the dots on a balloon when you blow it up. If this is true, are galaxies moving farther apart in the universe or closer together? Explain your answer.

19   Adaptations
Life Science

Did you know that when a polar bear hunts for a seal, it sometimes covers its nose with some snow or with its paw? Why do you think it does this? In what way is the polar bear well suited for hunting in the snow? List three other predators. For each, describe an adaptation that helps them catch their prey.

20   Balance
Physical Science

Place a ruler on a table so that part of it sticks out over the edge. Slowly move the ruler farther out over the edge. How far can you move it before it falls? Why do you think the ruler eventually falls over?

Science Superstar: Do the activity again, but this time add an eraser. Where can you put the eraser so that the ruler can be moved farther out than before?

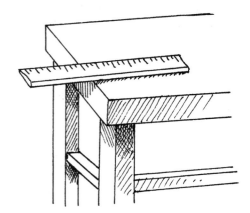

Daily Problems

21 Fossils

Suppose a construction company were building a new supermarket in your town. When the workers start digging, they begin to find fossil bones in the soil. The workers are in a hurry to finish the job and they want to ignore what they are finding. Write a letter giving the company at least two reasons why it should make an effort to preserve the fossils.

22 Hearing

Work with a partner. Stand in a quiet place with your eyes closed. Have your partner snap his or her fingers either in front of you, behind you, to your right, or to your left. Each time, guess where the sound is coming from. Do you always know where the sound is coming from? When is it hard to tell? Why do you think this is so?

23 Lasers

Have you ever seen a laser? If you have, describe where you saw it and what it looked like. Did you know that a laser beam consists of only one color of light? How is this different from sunlight or light from a light bulb? How do you think this makes laser beams more powerful? List three uses of lasers.

Science Superstar: Find out more about lasers. Write a paragraph describing what you learn.

24 Simple Machines

Did you know that the Egyptians built the great pyramids over 4,500 years ago? They didn't have modern equipment to help them build. Experts think that they used a simple machine to help them haul the big blocks of stone on top of one another. What machine do you think this was? Why did it make their work easier?

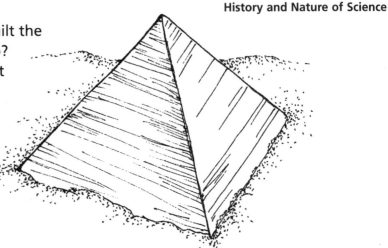

Daily Problems

25 Sound

Loop a rubber band around your thumbs. Then pluck the rubber band and listen to the sound. Loop the same rubber band around a small box. Pluck the band in the center of the open side. Which sound is louder? How do you explain this?

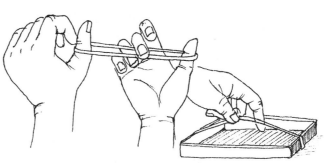

Science Superstar: Create different sounds by using different containers. Use identical rubber bands for each. Why do you think the sounds vary?

26 Space Travel

Do you think people will ever be able to fly to a planet in another solar system? Give three reasons to support your opinion.

27 The Skeletal System

Imagine your body with no bones! Draw a picture of what you think it would look like. How does your picture show an important function of the skeletal system?

Science Superstar: List five animals that have no bones. Which animals have body parts that act like bones? What are these body parts?

28 Sound on the Moon

Imagine you are on the Moon. You hit a rock with a hammer. Does the hammer make a sound when it hits the rock? Explain your answer.

Science Superstar: Find out how the astronauts on the Moon talked to one another.

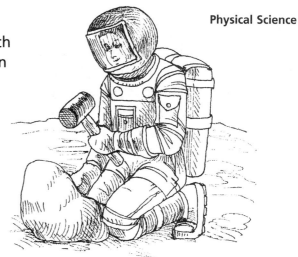

Daily Problems

29 Solar System

Earth and Space Science

In your lifetime, many space missions may be planned to investigate comets, asteroids, planets, their moons, and space beyond our solar system. Imagine that you are on a committee to decide what these missions will try to find out. List the three questions that interest you most. Tell why each question interests you.

30 Plant and Animal Processes

Human and Social Science

What do you have in common with a blade of grass? List all the ideas you can.

31 Lift

Science and Technology

Cut a strip of writing paper 2 inches by 11 inches. Hold the paper in front of your mouth and blow straight over it. What happens to the paper? Why do you think this happens? What part of an airplane do you think is designed on this principle?

32 Classifying Living Things

History and Nature of Science

The first modern system of classifying living things was developed in the 18th century by a Swedish botanist named Carolus Linnaeus. Today living things are divided into kingdoms. How many kingdoms do you think there are? Try to name them.

Daily Problems

33 Air Pressure

Imagine you are drinking soda through a straw. Suppose you have soda in the straw and you pull the straw out of the glass while holding your finger over its end. What do you think happens? If you took your finger off the end of the straw, what would happen then? How do you explain this?

34 Magnets

Work with a partner. While your partner is holding a sheet of paper, place a paper clip on top of it. Move a magnet beneath the paper. What happens? Try again, using a thicker kind of paper. Repeat the activity with other materials such as a book, a wooden board, or a glass dish.

Science Superstar: Predict how many thicknesses of paper you'd need in order to block the magnet's force. Then test your prediction.

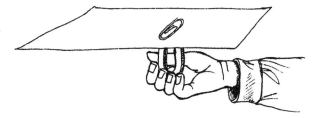

35 Adaptations

Choose a place in your classroom or outside. Then invent an imaginary animal that would blend into this place so it couldn't be easily seen. Draw a picture of the animal. Why would an animal need to blend in?

36 Buoyancy

Is it easier to float in the ocean or in a swimming pool? Here's how you can find out. Fill a tall drinking glass half full of water. Gently place an uncooked egg in it. What happens to the egg? Now add three tablespoons of salt and stir until it dissolves. Where is the egg now? What does this tell you?

Science Superstar: How could you find out the least amount of salt you could use for this activity?

Daily Problems

37 A Mystery Habitat

Earth and Space Science

You received a postcard from a friend. On the front there was a picture of a starfish. On the back your friend wrote, "We explored some really cool stuff today! We looked down between some rocks and saw sea anemones, mussels, and a crab." What kind of habitat was your friend exploring? How do you know? Name three other living things you'd expect to see in this habitat.

38 Tobacco

Human and Social Science

You and Lars are walking home from school. Suddenly Lars takes a pack of cigarettes out of his pocket. He offers you one. You refuse, but you are worried about Lars. List three things you could you tell him to persuade him not to smoke.

39 Artificial Body Parts

Science and Technology

The first artificial body part was probably a wooden leg. Today, the branch of medicine called *prosthetics* can provide many kinds of artificial body parts. What artificial body parts do you know about? What are they made of?

40 Your Calcium Needs

History and Nature of Science

Scientists used to think teenagers needed only 1,000 mg of calcium a day to stay healthy. Today they recommend that teenagers have about 1,200 mg of calcium in their diet every day. A glass of milk contains about 300 mg of calcium. How many glasses of milk would you have to drink each day to get the amount of calcium you need? Why is calcium important? What other foods are high in calcium?

Daily Problems

41 Genetics

Lucy and Fran are identical twins. What can you say about the DNA in their cells? Explain your reasoning.

42 Fossils

Have you ever seen a picture of a dinosaur with a long tail? Some dinosaurs walked with their tails in the air. Others walked with their tails on the ground. Explain how a paleontologist (a scientist who studies fossils) could tell whether a dinosaur dragged its tail on the ground.

43 Koalas

Have you ever seen koalas? If so, tell where you saw them and what they were doing. Some people think koalas are really bears. Give two reasons why they might think this. How are koalas different from bears?

Science Superstar: What type of animal are koalas? Where is their natural habitat? List two animals they are related to.

44 Light

Fill a drinking glass with water. Place a pencil in the glass. What do you observe? Why do you think this happens?

Science Superstar: Try this activity using different liquids, such as oil, soapy water, and salt water. What happens?

Daily Problems

45 Conservation

If more than three quarters of the Earth is covered with water, why is it so important not to waste water? List at least three things families can do at home to help conserve water.

46 Sight

This diagram shows the way the lens in the human eye focuses images on the retina. Why do you think you don't see everything upside down or really small?

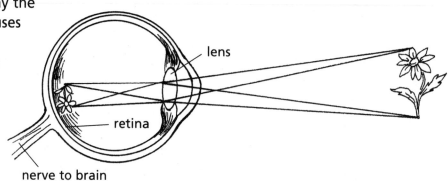

lens

retina

nerve to brain

47 Space Exploration

Imagine that you are Neil Armstrong, the first human to walk on the Moon. Write a journal entry for the day you stepped onto the Moon. You might include how you felt, what you saw, what you hoped to do, and any fears you had.

Science Superstar: Find out what Neil Armstrong's first words were when he stepped out of the spacecraft onto the lunar surface.

48 Adaptations

Would it surprise you to learn that bees have a way of "talking" to each other? More than 100 years ago, Karl von Frisch, an Austrian scientist, discovered that bees "dance" on the honeycomb inside their hive. One kind of dance tells other bees that flowers are near the hive. Another kind tells the bees that flowers are farther away, and points out the direction. How do you think this adaptation helps bees survive? Name another animal that has a way of "talking" and tell how it communicates.

Daily Problems

49 Reflections

Look at yourself in the bowl of a metal spoon. What do you notice? Then look at your reflection on the back of the spoon. What do you see? What do you think made the difference in the two reflections? Why do you think people use flat mirrors instead of curved mirrors in their bathrooms?

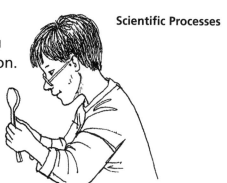

50 Biodiversity

Suppose someone says, "If you've seen one leaf, you've seen them all." What would you tell that person? Write what you'd say in a paragraph. Give specific details.

Science Superstar: Why is it important that there be differences among plants and animals, even within a single species?

51 Circulatory System

Imagine you are a drop of blood in the body. Draw or write a flow chart to show where you travel as you go from the heart, around the body, and back to the heart again.

52 Levers

Balance a ruler on a wooden block. Place a heavy book on one end of the ruler. Try lifting the book by pressing on the ruler at its other end. Then try lifting the book by pressing on the ruler close to the block. Which is easier? Why?

Science Superstar: Do you think you can hit a ball farther with your hand or with a bat? Explain your answer.

Daily Problems

53 Weather

How many different things can you find out from the weather page in your newspaper? Write down 10 things you can learn. Explain how five of them can be useful to you.

54 Sound

In social studies, Jill learned that Native Americans used to put their ears to the ground to listen for hoof beats. This helped them find out sooner if enemies were coming. How would you explain to Jill why this works? If she didn't believe you, how could you demonstrate it to her?

55 Space Exploration

The *Pathfinder* spacecraft landed on Mars on July 4, 1997. Maybe you have seen pictures of Mars sent back to Earth from *Pathfinder*. What does the Martian surface look like? What have we learned from pictures of Mars?

56 Hummingbird Populations

The very first hummingbirds lived in South America. From there they spread to Central America and North America. Find these places on a world map. Why do you think hummingbirds spread all over the Americas, but did not spread to Europe, Asia, Africa, or Australia?

Science Superstar: Why do you think most hummingbird feeders are red?

Daily Problems

57　Water in the Body

Did you know that your body is about two-thirds water? That means that if you weighed 90 pounds, about 60 pounds of that weight would be water! Weigh yourself or guess your weight. How many pounds of water are in your body? Suppose you wanted to find out how many 2-liter soda bottles you could fill with the amount of water that is in your body. How would you figure out the number of bottles you'd need?

58　Form and Function

Imagine you found these two skulls. Can you tell which one belonged to a plant-eater and which one belonged to a meat-eater? Explain how you know.

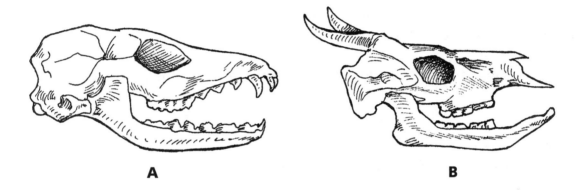

A　　　　　　　　　　　　　　　B

59　Recognizing Life

Pretend you are an astronaut in the year 2050. You land on a distant planet. You see a small object that you think might be a living thing. List three characteristics you would look for to help you decide. What equipment might help?

Science Superstar: Do you think there is intelligent life somewhere in the universe? Give your reasons.

60　Gravity

Imagine what the Earth would be like if there were no gravity. Write five things that would be different.

Daily Problems

61 Solar Eclipse

Can a small object block your view of a large object? To find out, crumple a small piece of paper into a ball about an inch across. Close one eye. With your open eye, look at a larger object while holding the paper ball a few inches in front of your open eye. What happens? Draw a diagram to show where the Earth, Moon, and Sun are during a solar eclipse. Explain why solar eclipses occur.

Science Superstar: If the Moon moves around the Earth about once a month, why do you think solar eclipses occur less than three times a year?

62 Alcohol

You've been asked to provide ideas for a poster about the dangers of alcohol. The poster will hang in school libraries. List ideas for three possible posters. For each, describe a picture and suggest a title to go with it.

Science Superstar: Decide which idea you like best and create the poster.

63 Cell Phones

Do you think people should bring cell phones on hiking or camping trips? Give three arguments that support your position. Then give three arguments that support the other point of view.

64 Respiratory System

You are having lunch with a friend. Suddenly, your friend starts choking on a piece of food. Why is this an emergency? What could you do to help?

Science Superstar: Henry Heimlich, an American doctor, figured out a way to help. Research the *Heimlich maneuver.* Describe how and why it works. Demonstrate the maneuver with a partner.

Daily Problems

65 Protective Coloration

Soldiers in the United States Army wear a mottled green and brown uniform for camouflage. Design an activity to find out how well the material works in different environments. Write exactly what you'd do.

66 Friction and Work

Friction is the force that makes it difficult to slide one surface over another. Sometimes it's useful to increase friction— for example, by spreading sand on icy roads to keep cars from sliding. Sometimes it's better to reduce friction—for example, by oiling moving parts on a bike so they don't rub against each other and cause damage.

Tell whether you would want to increase or reduce friction in the following situations and why:

• Two teams are playing ice hockey in a rink. The ice is all scratched up.

• Your old soccer shoes are worn and you keep slipping on the grass whenever you play soccer.

67 Animal Interactions

Michaela was looking through a gardening catalog. Among the seeds, fertilizers, and plants, she saw lifelike statues of falcons and owls for sale. "Why are these here?" she wondered. How would you explain this to her?

68 Cooling Down

It's a sunny day. Alyssa is getting hot and sweaty in the classroom. She takes her notebook and fans herself with it. She feels better right away. How does waving the book back and forth make Alyssa feel more comfortable?

Daily Problems

69 Comets

Halley's comet was seen on Earth in 1682, 1758, 1835, 1910, and 1986. What is a comet?

70 Cells

I am one of the smallest cells in the body. I am shaped like a disk. I live about three or four months, then I die. But before I die, I travel through the body many thousands of times. Sometimes I am bright red, sometimes I am dark red. What cell am I? Why does my color change? What is my most important function?

71 Computer Speech

Some people have to use a computer to speak for them. New software can make a computer "voice" sound like a real human voice. Without changing your voice at all say, "Please call the police right away." Now say it again as if there is an emergency. How did your voice change? How do you show emotion with your voice? Why would you want a computer "voice" to show emotion?

72 Light and Sound

Pretend you are a TV reporter about to interview the great American inventor Thomas Edison. Write a paragraph that will introduce him to the audience. Then write three questions you would ask him. Where could you look to find information about Thomas Edison?

Daily Problems

73 Molecules of Water

Scientific Processes

Fill a bowl with water. Then shake some pepper on top. You should be able to see the pepper floating on the water's thin "skin." Now wet your finger and rub it on a bar of soap. Touch your finger to the water. What happens to the pepper? Why do you think this happens?

74 Recycled Air

Scientific Thought

Have you ever wondered why the air we breathe never seems to get used up? One reason is that plants and animals recycle (reuse) the gases they need to survive. Animals and people breathe in oxygen and breathe out carbon dioxide. Plants, on the other hand, take in carbon dioxide and give off oxygen. This helps keep up the supply of gases that living things need. Do you think the oxygen you're breathing is the same oxygen breathed by dinosaurs millions of years ago? Explain your answer.

75 Classifying

Life Science

Keneesha's parents are opening a pet store. They plan to put the warm-blooded animals in the front of the store and the cold-blooded animals in the back. They've ordered these animals. Which will go in front and which in back?

cat   goldfish   snake   iguana

dog   turtle   parakeet   rabbit

List at least three other pets Keneesha's parents might sell in their store. Tell where they'd put each one.

76 Morse Code

Physical Science

In Morse code, combinations of dots and dashes stand for letters of the alphabet (for example • — stands for *a*, and — • • • stands for *b*). Work with a partner. Think of objects you could use to make different sounds that stand for dots and dashes. (Example: short and long finger taps)

Science Superstar: Research Morse code. Find out the code for all the letters of the alphabet. Practice sending messages back and forth with a partner.

Daily Problems

77 Crystals

Sprinkle a little table salt on a piece of dark paper. Look at it with a magnifying glass. Describe what you see. A crystal is a solid that has a regular shape because of the pattern of its atoms. Is salt a crystal? Why?

78 Sight

Draw two large dots about four inches apart on a sheet of paper. With one hand, hold the paper in front of you. With the other hand, cover your right eye. Stare at the dot on the left side of the paper with your right eye while moving the paper slowly toward you. What happens? Repeat with the opposite eye. What happens? What have you learned about the human eye that explains this, or how could you find out?

79 Electricity

Look around your classroom or your home. Name five things that use electricity. If there were no electricity, which of those things could you replace with something that doesn't need electricity? What would replace them?

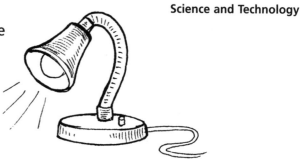

80 Extinction

Imagine dinosaurs wandering around the Earth millions of years ago. One day a huge asteroid crashes into the Earth. Everywhere the air is filled with soot and dust. Sunlight cannot get through to the ground. These thick clouds of soot and dust last for a very long time. What do you think happened to plants? What about the weather? What do you think could have happened to the dinosaurs?

Daily Problems

81 Skeletal and Respiratory Systems

Feel your sides. Can you feel your ribs? You have 12 ribs on each side of your body. The ribs are connected to your backbone, forming a cage around your chest cavity. Now breathe deeply with your hands on your sides. Can you feel your ribs move?

Think about what your ribs look like and where they are located. How do you think they help the body?

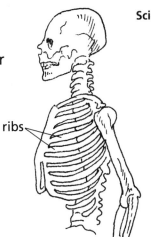

ribs

82 Adaptations—Ducks

Use two balloons and a basin or a sink half-filled with water. Blow up one of the balloons and tie a knot at the end. Now put both balloons in the basin and try to push them under the water. What do you observe? How does this explain the purpose of the air sacs in ducks' bodies? List two other adaptations that help ducks survive in their environment.

83 Characteristics of Plants

What is your favorite kind of tree? Write a letter to the tree. Tell the tree what you like about it. Describe how it helps you personally and how it helps the planet in general. Ask the tree three questions about itself.

Science Superstar: Pretend you are the tree. Write a letter back that answers your questions. If necessary, do research to find the answers.

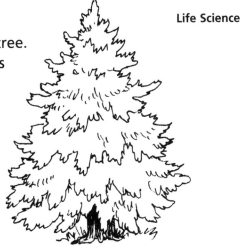

84 Carrying a Load

Gretchen is going to walk to school. She has to carry a heavy load of books. Will it be easier for her to carry the books in a backpack or in one hand in a book bag? Why?

Daily Problems

85 Climate
Earth and Space Science

Suppose a first-grader asks you why it is cold at the North and South poles and hot at the equator. How could you explain this using a piece of paper, a pencil, and a ruler? How could you explain it using a flashlight and a globe?

86 Fooling Our Eyes
Human and Social Science

Use cardboard, a pen, a pencil, and transparent tape. Cut two small squares out of the cardboard. With your pen or a dark crayon, draw pictures like the ones shown here. Attach the cardboard squares to the pencil so that the pictures face out. Roll the pencil back and forth between your palms as rapidly as you can. What do you see? Why do you think this happens? What do you see if you roll the pencil very slowly?

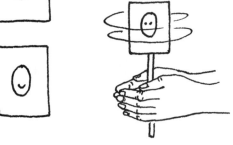

Science Superstar: What inventions depend on this ability of human vision?

87 Atoms
Science and Technology

What is an atom? What are its parts? How could you find out?

Science Superstar: Draw a picture of an atom. Label its parts. Then answer these questions: What does it mean to split an atom? When did scientists first learn to split an atom? Why would we want to split atoms?

88 Electricity
History and Nature of Science

Benjamin Franklin attached a metal rod to a kite. Then he tied a metal key to the kite string, which he held in his hand. He flew the kite during a thunderstorm. What do you think he was trying to find out? Why was his experiment extremely dangerous?

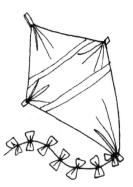

Daily Problems

89 Food Webs

Did you know that there are some animals that depend on each other for food? Owls and raccoons are an example. Owls eat baby raccoons. Big raccoons eat owl eggs. Make a drawing to show how you would illustrate this relationship in a food web.

90 Force

Have you ever noticed a crack in a driveway or sidewalk? List three possible causes for such cracks. If there are any cracks in the driveway or sidewalk near your house, what do you think caused them? Why do you think so?

91 Sense of Touch

Did you know that you have millions of touch sensors all over your body? These sensors let you feel things. Your skin is most sensitive where the sensors are close together and least sensitive where the sensors are far apart. Here's one way to check where the sensors are close together or far apart. Tape two pencils together. Make sure their points are even. Ask a partner to close his or her eyes. Then *gently* touch the points to different places along your partner's arm, hands, and fingertips. After each touch, ask how many points your partner felt. Based on this activity, where do you think the touch sensors are closest?

92 Levers

At recess, Rod and Susan climbed on opposite ends of the see-saw while their friends watched. Susan's end moved up into the air while Rod's end bumped down to the ground. What two things could the children do to balance the see-saw?

Science Superstar: Use a ruler, a quarter, a stack of pennies, and a narrow, rectangular block to demonstrate how each of your suggestions works.

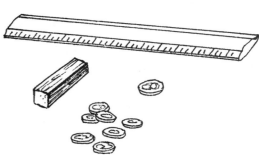

Daily Problems

93　Fossil Clues

Steven and Mark are walking along a path at the bottom of a cliff. Mark looks up and sees fossil shells in the layers of rock. He says, "We're not near the ocean, so how could there be shells here?" Steven isn't surprised at all. What does he understand that Mark doesn't? What type of rock are Mark and Steven probably looking at?

94　Good Posture

Stand against a wall in a normal position. Does the back of your head touch the wall? How about your shoulders? Buttocks? Heels? If not, adjust your body so they do. Now you have the correct posture for standing or walking! How does it feel? List three reasons why good posture is important.

95　Weight in Space

Here is some information NASA supplied about *Sojourner*, the robot designed to move around the surface of Mars:

Size　　　　　　2 feet × 1$\frac{1}{2}$ feet × 1 foot

Speed　　　　　16 inches a minute

Weight on Earth　34.2 pounds

Weight on Mars　23 pounds

Explain why NASA gives two different weights but only one size.

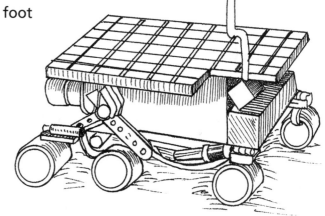

96　Careers

Do you ever wonder what you will be when you grow up? When your great-grandparents were children, they probably didn't dream of becoming astronauts when they grew up. Why didn't they? Think of an imaginary job that does not exist now but that might exist in the future. How could the job involve science? Write a paragraph describing it.

Daily Problems

97 Form and Function

Scientific Processes

Did you know that some fish are transparent? You can see right through them. Why would a transparent body be useful if you lived in the water? List three other ways fish are adapted to living in water.

98 Aging

Scientific Thought

Imagine you are at the park and you see people of all ages. How can you tell who are the youngest and who are the oldest? List five ways. Why can't you judge a person's age by looks alone?

99 Interactions

Life Science

Suppose that your house has termites. The exterminator tells your family that there are two ways to get rid of them. One is to use chemicals to kill them. The other is to freeze the termites using a very cold liquid. Before you decide what to do, what else would you want to know? Write three or more questions you'd ask the exterminator.

100 Periscopes and Reflections

cardboard tube   Physical Science

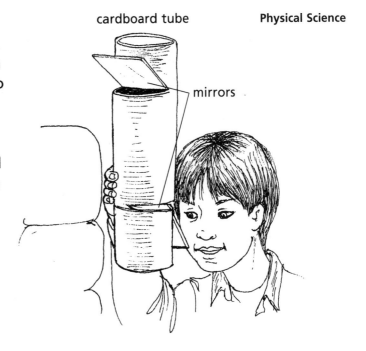

mirrors

Tim was too short to see over the wall in front of his house. To help him, he built a periscope. Draw a diagram with arrows to show how it would work. How could Tim use his periscope to see around corners?

Science Superstar: If you have a tube and two small mirrors, try making a periscope of your own.

Daily Problems

101 Day and Night
Earth and Space Science

Mario lives in Chicago. His dog Sparky goes to sleep when it gets dark and wakes up at sunrise. Next June, Mario's family and Sparky will vacation in Alaska. If Sparky doesn't change his sleeping habits, will he sleep more or less in Alaska? Explain your answer.

102 A Zigzag Course
Human and Social Science

Have you ever ridden a bike up a steep hill? If you have, then you know that it helps to go up the hill using a zigzag motion. Explain why a person would choose to travel a zigzag course rather than ride straight up a hill. How are hiking trails and mountain roads designed to handle mountains? Why?

103 Artificial Intelligence
Science and Technology

Have you ever played a game against a machine? In 1997, a computer won a chess match against the greatest chess player in the world! The computer had been programmed to analyze 200 million chess moves each second. Do you think this means computers have become smarter than humans? Give at least two arguments to support your opinion.

104 Scientific Models
History and Nature of Science

Until recently, models of dinosaurs showed scaly skin, like a reptile's. Now scientists know that the skin of at least one dinosaur was made up of small bumps about a half inch across and an eighth of an inch high. Each bump had grooves from top to bottom. You can be sure that some dinosaur models will look a bit different now!

Why do you think scientists knew how dinosaurs were shaped but not what their skin looked like? What do you think happened that led scientists to think that their models were not accurate? Why do you think scientific models change?

Daily Problems

105 Muscles

Do you think you can hold a pencil at arm's length for 20 minutes? Time yourself and try it. How long were you able to hold the pencil? How do you explain what happens? Are you surprised at the result? How can you increase the strength and endurance of muscles?

106 Adaptations

This table shows the major achievements in human history.

4–10 million years ago	Walks on two feet
2 million years ago	Intelligence develops
1.8 million years ago	Uses tools and fire
60,000 years ago	Language develops
30,000 years ago	Lives in communities

Imagine that you're a scientist looking at the achievements of the 20th century. What would you write as a major human achievement of this time? Write a paragraph to explain your choice.

107 Adaptations—Birds

If you weighed yourself with wet clothes on, would you weigh more or less than if your clothes were dry? Why? Now imagine you're a bird flying in the rain. Why doesn't your body get soggy and heavy? Explain your reasoning. In what other ways are birds adapted for flying?

108 Physical Changes

Pretend you are a drop of water. You used to be in the ocean. Now you are on land. How did you get there? How will you get back to the ocean?

Daily Problems

109 Flood Control

Suppose you live in an area that sometimes floods. You are part of a group that is planning future developments in your community. You want to convince the group that it is important to keep land that has trees and shrubs. How could you demonstrate that land with plants is better protected against floods than paved land?

110 Sounds

A *decibel* is a unit for measuring the loudness of sound. Sounds louder than 85 decibels can damage your hearing. Which sounds on this list do you hear frequently? List three ways you can protect yourself against hearing loss.

Breathing	10 decibels
People whispering	20 decibels
People talking	50–70 decibels
Heavy traffic	80 decibels
A food blender	90 decibels
Loud rock music	110 decibels
A jet engine	140 decibels

111 Nocturnal Animals

Animals that come out at night are called *nocturnal*. Scientists use night vision goggles to learn more about nocturnal animals. Night vision goggles amplify (make greater) what little light there is, so you can see animals and other things in the dark. Name three animals you would like to study with night vision goggles. What things could you find out?

112 Function of the Heart

What does the heart do? Does it surprise you that the answer to this question stumped scientists for centuries? Some thought the heart warmed the blood. Then about 400 years ago, William Harvey, an English doctor, found out the purpose of the heart. Write one question that puzzles scientists today. Do you think future scientists will be surprised that today's scientists can't answer this question? Why or why not?

Daily Problems

113   Animals with Blubber

Scientific Processes

Some animals have blubber, a thick layer of fat that lies under the skin. To find out why, get two cups of ice water. Completely cover one index finger with petroleum jelly or vegetable shortening. Then put both of your index fingers in the ice water, one in each cup. Wait 30 seconds. Describe how each finger feels and tell why you think it feels that way. Think of an animal with blubber. Tell how blubber helps this animal.

114   Weather

Scientific Thought

Here's how to figure out how far away lightning is. First count the number of seconds between the flash and when you hear the thunder. Then divide the number by 5. The answer gives you the number of miles away the lightning is. Now practice. If you count 5 seconds between the flash and the thunder, how far away is the lightning? If you count 10 seconds, how far away is it? If you count 2 seconds, how far away is it?

Science Superstar: Explain why this works.

115   Body's Response to Fear

Life Science

Have you ever seen a cat arch its back when it's frightened? What happens to the hair on a cat's body when it's scared? How do you think this makes it look to its enemies? Now think about a time when you were frightened. Did you notice goose bumps on your skin? What do you think causes goose bumps?

116   Energy

Physical Science

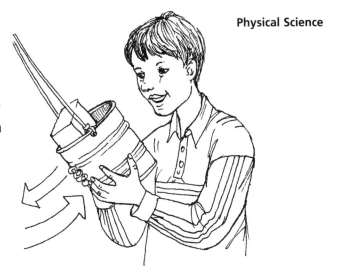

Suppose you were the child in this picture. If you let go of the can, would you have to get out of the way to avoid being hit when it swung back in your direction? Why or why not? Suppose you pushed the can away from you instead of just letting it go. Would that change your answer? Explain.

Daily Problems

117   Meteorology

Get a clear drinking glass. Fill it about half full of ice cubes. Take a deep breath, then exhale into the glass. Can you see the "cloud"? Why do you think this happens? Now imagine yourself walking outside. On what kind of day can you "make a cloud" by blowing a breath out into the air?

118   Sight

Roll a sheet of paper into a tube. Keeping both eyes open, put the tube up to your right eye and look through it at a distant object. Hold your left hand up, palm facing you. What do you see? How do you explain this? Try this activity holding up other things besides your hand. Describe what happens. What happens if you look through the tube at objects closer or farther away?

119   Avoiding Bone and Muscle Injuries

Have you ever played computer or video games for so long that your muscles ached when you got up? *Ergonomics* is the science of designing objects like desks, chairs, and computer keyboards so people can use them for long periods without hurting themselves. Think of two things you can do to make working at a computer easier on your body, even if you don't have ergonomic equipment.

120   Lucky Accidents

Do you know how nerves deliver messages around the body? The first person who had a clue about this was Luigi Galvani, an Italian professor. He had cut open the leg of a frog for an experiment. By chance, he put a machine that made electrical sparks near the frog's leg. The leg suddenly moved. He went on to prove that electricity caused the movement. Now we know that nerves carry electrical messages to muscles. Name another discovery that resulted from a lucky accident. What have you learned by chance when you were studying something else?

Daily Problems

121 Seeds

Design a way to find out if seeds will sprout as well in the dark as they do in the light. Then design a way to see if seeds will sprout as well in a cold place as in a warm place. Write the procedures for both experiments. What results do you predict?

Science Superstar: Carry out the experiments. Keep records. Graph the results.

122 Getting Drinking Water

Imagine that your ship has broken apart in a storm. You are floating at sea in a life raft. The water is calm and it's a sunny day. You have no drinking water. You do have a plastic bag, a small metal bowl, and a rubber band. How can you get drinking water? Why not drink the ocean water?

Science Superstar: Try out your plan. Describe the results.

123 Classification

Susie thinks a seal is a fish. Her friend, Anna, thinks it's a mammal. Who do you think is right? Give three reasons for your answer.

124 Magnetism

Suppose you have a glass of water. An iron nail and a plastic button are at the bottom of the glass. You also have a magnet. You want to get the nail out of the glass without getting your fingers wet and without pouring any water out. What could you do? Could you get the button out of the glass the same way? Explain.

Daily Problems

125   Uses of Rocks

Timmy has just moved to a new house. The kitchen counter is made of granite. What kind of rock is granite? Why is it a good choice for a kitchen counter? Make a list of other ways rocks are used for building.

126   Mushrooms

You and your friend Ali are hiking in the woods. Ali notices some mushrooms growing under a tree. She says, "Let's pick these and eat them." What should you do? Why?

Science Superstar: What type of living things are mushrooms? Why are they important to the forest?

127   Problems of Technology

A factory in your hometown has been dumping harmful chemicals into the river. Write a letter to the newspaper saying why this should be stopped. Give at least three reasons.

128   Skeletal and Muscular Systems

Did you know that the Achilles tendon gets its name from an ancient Greek myth? When Achilles was a baby, his mother dipped him in magic water. After this, no one could hurt his body where the water had touched it. But his mother had held Achilles by his ankles. The water didn't touch his body where her hands were. Eventually Achilles was killed by an arrow that pierced the tendon connected to his heel. Why is this tendon, called the Achilles tendon, so important? What does it do? What do you think would happen to you if your Achilles tendon were cut or torn?

Achilles tendon

Daily Problems

129 Evaporation
Scientific Processes

Have you ever stepped out of a warm bath and felt cold? To find out why, try this activity. Turn on the faucet. Adjust it until the water feels warm to the touch, but is not too hot to put your hand in. Hold your right hand in the water until it feels much warmer than your left hand. Now take your hand out of the water. Don't dry it with a towel. Let it dry in the air. As it dries, which hand feels warmer? How do you explain this?

Science Superstar: Explain why perspiring is one of the body's important adaptations.

130 Animal Behavior
Scientific Thought

Pretend that you have a pet bird. Design an activity to find out if a change in bird food might have an effect on the behavior of your bird.

131 Adaptations—Caribou
Life Science

Caribou live in snowy regions. They have broader hooves than many other members of the deer family. This activity will show you why. Get a new crayon and a piece of clay. Flatten the clay. Using the pointed end of the crayon, lightly press down to make it "walk" across the clay. Then do the same thing using the flat end of the crayon. Use the same pressure as you did before. Now examine the "footprints." How do your results explain why caribou have broad hooves?

132 Levers
Physical Science

Use a ruler, the edge of your desk, and an eraser or paper clip to show how a lever works. Draw your machine.

Science Superstar: Label your machine. Which part is the fulcrum? Which part is the load?

Daily Problems

133 Wind and Air

Use a tall plastic or metal container at least four inches across the top. (An empty quart yogurt carton or coffee can will work.) Fill the container half full of water. Look down into the center of the container as you slowly stir the water with a spoon. What happens? See if you can make this happen all the way to the bottom. What do you notice about the water at the sides of the container? What events in nature does this activity remind you of?

134 Skin Safety

Why do doctors warn people against staying out too long in the sun? List four ways you can protect yourself from the sun.

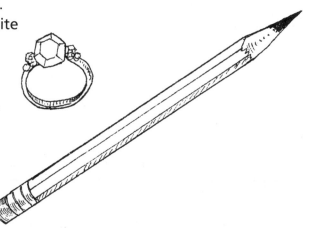

135 Keeping Warm

List three ways you can warm yourself up when you are cold. Explain why each way works. Make a list of some inventions that help keep you warm.

136 Atoms and Elements

Write two adjectives that describe a diamond. Now write two adjectives that describe graphite (the "lead" in pencils). Surprisingly, diamond and graphite are both natural forms of the very same element—carbon. In 1773, Antoine Lavoisier burned both graphite and diamond. The gas they gave off was exactly the same, proving that they were the same element. What do you think explains the difference in the way diamond and graphite look?

Daily Problems

137 Magnetic Force
Scientific Processes

Pretend you have a bar magnet, a sewing needle, and five paper clips. How could you show that magnetism can be transferred from one object to another? How could you show that magnetic force can pass through a series of objects?

Science Superstar: Gather the materials. Try out your plans.

138 Electricity
Scientific Thought

Paul says the light bulb in both pictures will light. Mary says only the light bulb in picture **A** will light. Who is right? Explain your answer.

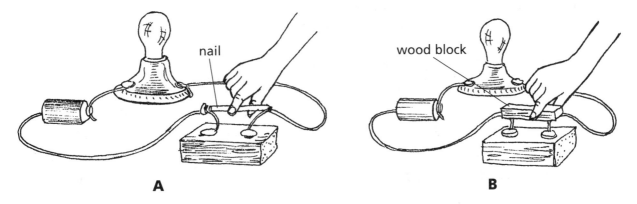

A   **B**

139 Reverence for Life
Life Science

Albert Schweitzer spent much of his life helping the sick. He also cared for animals. He believed that all living things—plants, animals, and people—were important. He called this idea "reverence for life." Imagine a butterfly flies into your room. How could you show "reverence for life"?

140 Simple Machines
Physical Science

Joshua needed to make a list of simple machines. He wrote the word *lever* and underneath it, he wrote *scissors* and *clothespins*. What other simple machines could Joshua put on his list? Which of these machines have you used?

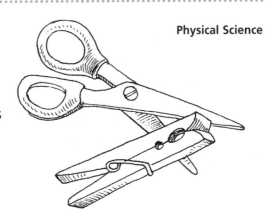

Daily Problems

141 Wind and Speed

Earth and Space Science

Myra and her parents live in California. Her grandparents live in New Jersey. When Myra visits her grandparents, the pilot of the airplane announces that the flying time to New Jersey is five and a half hours. But on the way back from New Jersey to California, the pilot announces that the flying time is six and a half hours. How can you explain this?

142 Animal Interactions

Human and Social Science

On a walk through the woods, Riley and Erwin came across a fawn (a baby deer). Riley said it probably had been abandoned by its mother. He wanted to take it home. Erwin didn't think that was a good idea. He told Riley not to touch it. Who do you think was right? Explain why you think so. What could Riley and Erwin have done to decide what was best for the fawn?

143 Properties of Materials

Science and Technology

Suppose you cooked hot cereal in two different metal pans. One pan had a rubber handle. The other pan had a metal handle. Which pan would you have to be more careful with? Why?

144 Immunization

History and Nature of Science

Do you remember getting vaccinations to protect you against certain diseases? List four diseases you probably won't get because you have been vaccinated.

Science Superstar: The very first vaccination for human disease was developed by the Englishman, Edward Jenner, in 1796. Do you know what the disease was? How could you find out?

Weekly Puzzlers

1 Vertebrates

Scientific Processes

If you know that an animal is a vertebrate, what do you know about it? Scientists classify living things into groups. The members of each group share certain traits and characteristics. Each group can be divided into subgroups. Find out what the five main classes of vertebrates are. Then prepare an exhibit of these five classes. Use pictures from books and magazines or make drawings to include in your display.

2 Water Colors

Scientific Thought

Have you ever mixed different colors of water to get new colors? Sometimes the results can be quite muddy. Here's a fun way to mix colors and unmix them if you don't like the result!

Get food coloring and three clear glass jars or bottles. Fill each jar with water. Add food coloring to make one jar of water yellow, one red, and one blue. Now position the jars in front of one another and look through them at the same time. Overlap all the possible combinations, including three colors at once. Make a chart to record the results of your color mixes.

Try reversing the color you look through first. Try adding more color to one jar to deepen its color. Do these variations make a difference in your results? If so, what is the difference?

Weekly Puzzlers

3 Breakdown

Have you ever wondered what happens to wild plants and animals when they die? To find out, choose a few pieces of leftover food, such as a banana peel, bread crusts, or bits of meat. Sprinkle them with water and seal them in separate self-sealing plastic bags. Watch the bags for about a week, but don't open them again. Describe what happens in the bags, then discard them.

Science Fair Tip: For a project on how temperature affects decomposition, repeat what you did. But this time, place an identical set of bags in the refrigerator. Compare your results at the end of two weeks.

4 Attraction Reaction

What materials will stop the attraction of a magnet? Does the thickness of the material make a difference? Does the strength of the magnet affect your results? Design a way to find out the answers to these questions. Carry out your plan. Record what you do and the results of each part of your investigation. Then write your conclusions.

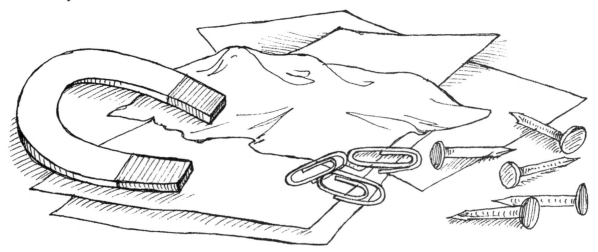

Weekly Puzzlers

5   It's the Greatest!

What do you think is the greatest invention of all time? How could you find out more about it? Who invented it? When was it invented? Make a sketch or write a paragraph telling why you think the invention is so great. If it had never been invented, how would our lives be different?

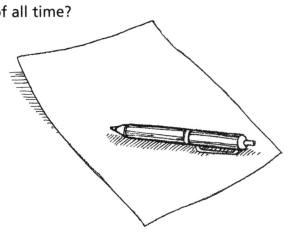

6   Up and Down

Does your height change during the day? If you think so, predict *how* it will change. Then ask someone at home to help you measure your height at the beginning and end of each day for four days.

Each time you take a measurement, fill in a chart like the one below

	Day 1	Day 2	Day 3	Day 4
Morning				
Evening				

Look at your results. What do you notice? What part of your skeletal system do you think changes to give you these results?

Science Superstar: Repeat the investigation. This time record your activities on each day. Do your activities seem to make a difference? If so, how?

Weekly Puzzlers

7 Wish You Were Here

How does the weather where you live compare to the weather in other places? Look in the weather section of your newspaper. Find the names of four cities you'd like to visit. Find the city you live in or one close to it. Compare yesterday's highest and lowest temperatures in all five cities. Which city had the greatest temperature range (the difference between the highest and lowest temperature)? Why do you think there was a range in temperature?

Science Superstar: Use two colors to make a graph of the high and low temperatures for each city you chose. Would you say the cities with the warmest high temperatures also have the warmest low temperatures? Use your graph to support your answer.

8 Adventures in Space

Do you know the highlights of space exploration? On each date on the timeline below, an important event took place in the history of space exploration. Find out what happened on each date. Copy the timeline and write in the events that occurred. Then put the year of your birth on the timeline. What adventures in space have happened in your lifetime?

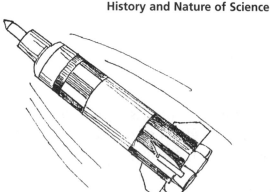

1961   1965   1969   1986   1990   1997

Weekly Puzzlers

9 Fade Out

Use construction paper or newspaper for this investigation. Place the paper in sunlight. Put a few small objects on it, such as buttons, paper clips, or pencils. Leave it in the sun for the whole day. Then remove the objects. What do you notice? Is this a chemical change or a physical change? What is your reasoning?

Science Superstar: Name two other ways you could change the paper—one chemical and one physical.

10 Water Works

How do rivers affect land? This activity lets you find out. You'll need a sheet of heavy cardboard (about 12" × 18"), a pitcher of water, a flower pot, a trowel, and some soil.

1. Cover the cardboard with a layer of damp soil. Form mounds of dirt to make "hills."

2. Rest one end of the cardboard against the flower pot to form a slope.

3. Slowly pour water on the upper end of the cardboard. Watch how the water affects the "land."

What happened when you poured the water over the soil? What can you say about how rivers affect the landscape?

Weekly Puzzlers

11   Experimenting with Leaves

Scientific Processes

What would happen to you if someone clamped
your mouth shut and put tape over your nose?
You can create this same situation in the leaves
of a houseplant. Get a potted geranium. Spread
petroleum jelly on both sides of two leaves.
Watch the plant for two weeks. How do the
leaves with petroleum jelly compare with
the other leaves? Why do you think this
happened?

Science Superstar: Read about *photosynthesis*.
Which raw material has failed to reach the cells
in the leaves you treated?

12   All Thumbs

Human and Social Science

How important are your thumbs? To find out, try not using them. First ask
someone to tape your thumbs close to your palms. (This works best if you wrap
the tape all around your hand.) Then try the simple tasks below. For each one,
report whether you were able to do the activity. If you were able to do it, tell
what you did.

1. drink from a cup

2. throw a ball

3. eat with a fork

4. pick up a grape

5. turn a doorknob

6. tie your shoelaces

What do you conclude? Is it
possible to do the tasks without thumbs?
Does it take much more effort? How do you think civilization
would be different if people had developed without thumbs?

Weekly Puzzlers

13   Sky Colors

Have you ever wondered why the sky is blue during the day? The sky is made up of gas molecules and dust. You can make a model to find out where the color of the sky comes from.

Get a tall glass jar, water, one teaspoon of milk, and a flashlight. You'll also need a darkened room.

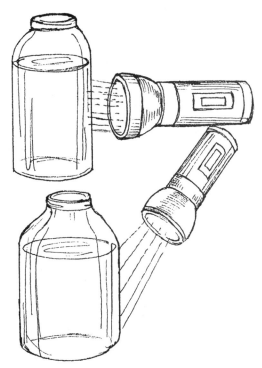

To make a model of the atmosphere, fill the jar with water and stir in the milk. The molecules of milk are like the dust particles in the sky. In a darkened room, shine the flashlight directly at the side of the jar. Then shine the flashlight from an angle.

What do you notice about the colors of the "sky"? What does the flashlight represent? Sunlight contains all the colors of the rainbow. When sunlight is split into various colors, the colors we see depend on which colors are reflected and which are absorbed. Why do you think we see blue skies during the day and red skies at sunrise or sunset?

14   Cooling Down

What do you think happens to air when it gets cold? You can find out with a balloon and some string. Blow up the balloon and knot it tightly. Use a string or tape measure to measure the distance around it. Put the balloon in the freezer for a couple of hours, then measure it again. What do you observe? How do you explain what happens?

Science Superstar: Find out what happens to a balloon filled with water if you put it in the freezer for a couple of hours.

Weekly Puzzlers

15 Safety First

What should you think about if you are making a safety sign like STOP or SHARK WARNING? Design a way to find out which colors can be most easily seen from a distance. Test your plan. Write your results. How else can you use this information?

Science Superstar: Design a way to find out which colors can be most easily seen at night. Test your plan. Write your conclusions.

16 Here Today, Gone Tomorrow

Did you know that at least two-thirds of all the medicines used today first came from rain forest plants? Do research to learn more about rain forests.

1. Tell what rain forests are and where they are located.

2. Give three more reasons why rain forests are so important.

3. Give two reasons why rain forests are disappearing.

4. Give three more interesting facts about rain forests.

Weekly Puzzlers

17   Star Light, Star Bright

Scientific Processes

Do you think a weak source of light will look farther away than a strong source of light, even when you look at them from the same distance? Design an activity to find out. Test your plan. Report your conclusions. What do your conclusions tell you about the distance of the stars you see in the sky?

18   A Tricky Problem

Scientific Thought

Fill a soda bottle (or any other narrow-necked bottle) half full of water. Add about an inch of oil to the water in the bottle. What happens? Why? You may have seen this demonstration before. But here's a puzzle for you. How can you pour just the water out of the bottle without first pouring off the oil? When you think you have a method, try it and see if it works. Be sure to use a basin so that if it doesn't work, you can use a funnel to put the liquids back in the bottle. Then you can try again.

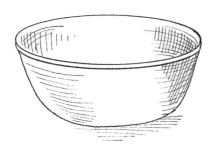

Weekly Puzzlers

19 Water Wonders

Life Science

How does water move from the roots of plants up to the leaves? Try this activity and find out.

1. Get a stalk of celery that has a lot of leaves on top. Cut off the bottom so that the whole stalk is about 10 inches long.

2. Carefully cut the stem in half lengthwise. Stop at about the middle of the stem.

3. Put each half of the stem in a separate glass. Add about two inches of water to each glass. Add red food coloring to one glass and blue food coloring to the other.

4. Leave the celery overnight. Then record your observations.

What did you observe? Did the results surprise you? Look carefully at the bottom of the stalk. What do you see? What has this activity shown you about how water moves through a stem?

20 Colors and Heat

Human and Social Science

On a hot, sunny day, place two identical ice cubes in identical dishes or bowls. Take them outside and put them in the sun. Sprinkle one of the ice cubes lightly with dark dirt. Then watch the ice cubes as they melt. What do you observe? Why does this happen? Why is it important to use identical ice cubes and identical bowls in this activity? Now think about the results you got. If you wanted to keep cool on a hot, sunny day, why would light clothing be a better choice than dark clothing?

Weekly Puzzlers

21 Mystery Fossil

Paleontologists are scientists who study fossils. Imagine that a paleontologist has just discovered four pieces of a mystery fossil. How hard would it be to fit the pieces together? You could demonstrate by designing an activity in which a person has to piece a "fossil" together. Ask someone to help you test your idea. You could use bones that are left over from a chicken dinner, or you could use jigsaw puzzles or other items to create the four pieces of the fossil. How could you find out if it is harder to reconstruct the fossil if one of the pieces is missing?

Science Fair Tip: Find out how paleontologists work. Prepare a display about what they do.

22 Take a Deep Breath

About how much air do your lungs hold? To find out, you'll need a half-gallon jar, a big basin or pot, water, a piece of paper, a straw, and a helper.

1. Fill the basin or pot half full of water. Fill the jar full of water.

2. Put a piece of paper over the top of the jar. Then hold your hand over the paper and tip the jar into the container of water. Remove the paper. The jar should be upside down and still full of water.

3. Ask your helper to lift the jar a few inches but not to let it come above the top of the water.

4. Take a deep breath. Then blow the air in your lungs out through the straw and into the basin of water. Make sure the far end of the straw is under the opening of the jar.

What happened? How can you tell how much air was in your lungs? Why isn't this an exact measure of how much air your lungs hold?

Weekly Puzzlers

23 Keeping Warm

Scientific Thought

What will keep you warmer on a cold day—wearing many thin layers or wearing one thick layer? Design an investigation to find out. Figure out a way to do this investigation even when it isn't cold outside.

24 Heads Up

History and Nature of Science

The earliest fossil footprints showing that humans walked on two feet are more than 3 million years old! They were found by the archeologist Mary Leakey in Tanzania. What do you think these early humans looked like?

Walk on all fours like a dog or a cat. Try it for a couple of minutes, then answer these questions.

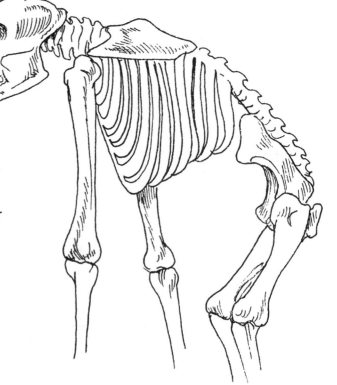

1. What are some things you can't do as easily?

2. What are some things you can't do at all?

3. How does walking on two feet change the way you see the environment around you?

4. When you are outside and walking on four limbs, does more or less sun land on you? How would this affect you?

5. How do you think civilization would be different if humans never walked upright?

Weekly Puzzlers

25 Soundproofing

Have you ever tried having a private talk with a friend when family members were in different rooms of your home? If you have, then you know that sound carries. If you were building a soundproof room, what materials could you use? You can test materials on a small scale to find out. Start with a small battery-operated radio and a cardboard box. Turn on the radio and place the box over it. Can you still hear the radio? Try lining the box with various materials, such as layers of newspaper, cloth, egg cartons, "popcorn" packing material, bubble wrap, cotton balls—whatever you can think of. Which material makes the box most soundproof?

26 Chemistry in Action

Get a small funnel. Put it in the top of a narrow-necked bottle. Add a tablespoon of baking soda. Then add one-half cup of vinegar. Remove the funnel and, as quickly as you can, put a balloon over the neck of the bottle. Describe what happens. Shake the bottle gently and see if anything more happens. Explain what you see.

Weekly Puzzlers

27 Parts of a Flower

Although flowers come in many shapes and colors, do you think they share common structures? Examine a real flower to find out. Study the flower carefully and compare it to the diagram. If possible, use a simple flower—one with a single row of petals.

1. Draw your flower. Label the main parts.

2. Are any parts missing? Which ones?

3. How are the stamens arranged? What color are they?

4. What color are the petals?

5. Pick up one stamen and rub its tip across a piece of paper. What do you see? What is this substance?

6. Take off the petals and the sepals. Then cut the pistil open the long way. Draw what you see. Does your flower have the parts you see in the drawing? Label the ones it has.

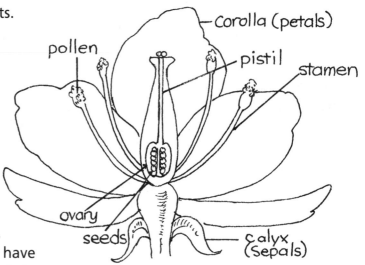

Science Fair Tip: Collect a variety of flowers. Examine them the way you examined the flower in this activity. Make a display of stamens, pistils, sepals, petals, and other flower parts.

28 Static Cling

Blow up a balloon. Rub it back and forth on your clothes about 20 times. Now see if it can pick up little pieces of paper. Rub it again and see if it will pick up eraser rubbings, hair, and other items. Will the balloon move a stream of water coming slowly from the sink? How do you explain what happens?

Science Fair Tip: Design and carry out an investigation to see if weather affects what happens. Report the results and write your conclusions.

Weekly Puzzlers

29 A Walk Through Time

This activity will help you picture the history of life on Earth.

Get a long rope, nine paper clips, some paper, and a pen. Stretch the rope along the edges of the playground until you have about 100 feet of rope. Then make labels of the events on this list and attach them at the correct points along the rope.

25 feet	first one-celled organisms
40 feet	first vertebrates in the ocean
51 feet	first land plants
62 feet	first vertebrates on land
70 feet	first dinosaurs
88 feet	first birds and mammals
99 feet, $10\frac{3}{4}$ inches	stone age people
99 feet, 11 inches	Columbus sails to America

How do you think scientists know when these events occurred? What does your "timeline" tell you about how long people have been on Earth?

30 In Danger

Find out if there is an endangered animal in your state. If there isn't one, choose an endangered animal from another area. Try to find out why the animal is endangered. Then see what, if anything, is being done to save it. Write about what you learn.

Weekly Puzzlers

31 Fingerprints

To see your fingerprint, you need a pencil, a piece of white paper, and some transparent tape. First rub a 2-inch square with a pencil until the square is filled in and quite dark. Then rub the pad of your left index finger over the square until your finger is dark. Press a piece of tape over that fingertip. Remove the tape and stick it onto the white paper. Compare your fingerprint with those of your classmates or people in your family. What do you notice? How do you think computers can help police officers identify people by their fingerprints?

Science Fair Tip: Find out what the three general patterns of fingerprints are. See what percent of your class has each type and how this compares with the population as a whole. Learn how fingerprinting is used by government agencies, banks, or other businesses in your community.

32 Puzzle Pieces

Find a map of the world. Trace North America, Africa, and South America. Cut out each continent. Pretend they are puzzle pieces whose edges have worn away. How would you fit them together? What do you notice about the shape of the coastlines? What do you think this means about the history of these continents?

Science Superstar: Find evidence that supports your hypothesis. To get started, research one of these topics: *Alfred Wegener, Continental Drift, Mid-Atlantic Ridge.* Write a paragraph that describes the evidence.

Weekly Puzzlers

33 If You Ran the Park

Imagine you were in charge of a National Park, such as Yosemite, Yellowstone, or Bryce Canyon. What kinds of rules would you make? Make a decision about each of the following issues. Give your reasons for each decision.

1. Do you think hikers should be allowed to wash clothes in natural lakes and streams?

2. Do you think backpackers should have to stay on the trails or should they be allowed to explore wherever they want?

3. Do you think cars should be banned from national parks?

Science Superstar: Do research on one of the National Parks. Find out what their rules are.

34 Digging Down

Get a paper cup, some dirt, and two bones. (Use bones that you've saved from dinner.) Make a model to show that when you dig down into the earth and come upon fossils, the one you dig up last is the one that was left there first.

Make a plan to alter your model so that someone else can see what is under the surface without digging into it. You may need to use additional materials. Try your plan and see if it works.

Weekly Puzzlers

35 Absolute Silence

Life Science

Tape five pennies to the bottom of each shoe. Then try to walk across an uncarpeted floor or a sidewalk without making any noise. What happens?

Ask someone in your family to stand with their eyes closed at least 12 feet away from you. Try to sneak up on them. Ask them to tell you when they hear you. How close did you get? Now take your shoes off and try again. How close did you get this time? How does this explain the value to tigers of the retractable claws and fur pads on the bottoms of their feet?

Science Fair Tip: Make a display about predators. Include information about the adaptations that help them catch the animals they hunt.

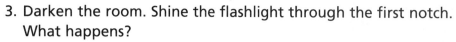

36 How Light Travels

Physical Science

You can demonstrate something important about light. You'll need a pair of scissors, some clay, four small index cards, and a flashlight.

1. In three of the cards, cut a notch like the one in the picture.

2. Use the clay to stand the notched cards up in a row. Adjust them so the notches line up. Stand the unnotched card up behind the rest.

3. Darken the room. Shine the flashlight through the first notch. What happens?

4. Move the cards so that the notches no longer line up. Now what happens when you shine the flashlight through the first notch?

What have you demonstrated about how light travels?

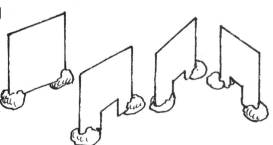

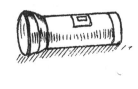

Answers

▼▼▼▼▼▼▼

DAILY PROBLEMS

DP 1: Sea life can become entangled in plastic trash. Without hands, animals can't free themselves. *Superstar:* 300 years.

DP 2: Metals expand when heated. *Superstar:* Use a damp cloth to hold the lid and get a better grip (the cloth increases friction); break the vacuum seal by banging the edge of the lid with the handle of a knife.

DP 3: All but the cat, blue jay, worm, and snail would be kept away.

DP 4: Lip feels warm. Possible reasons: Work is being done; friction creates heat.

DP 5: Possible answer: Mercury and Venus would be too hot, Mars too cold. *Superstar:* The closer to the Sun, the higher the surface temperature.

DP 6: Approximately 320 million. *Superstar:* Effects might include more pollution, longer lines at amusement parks, more crowded beaches.

DP 7: Technological advances have made smaller products possible. Benefits include portability, lower prices. Possible items: radios, computers.

DP 8: The balls landed at the same time.

DP 9: A milk formula. Whales are mammals—mammal mothers produce milk for babies.

DP 10: Beaver. Evidence: cut logs, lodge. Possible answer: Return at dusk when beavers are active and quietly watch the area.

DP 11: Seeds. Picture shows seed-eater's beak. Possible resources: Nature book, bird book, zoos, animal shelters.

DP 12: red—see green; green—see red; blue—see yellow; yellow—see blue. *Superstar:* Your eyes are able to detect color because of light-sensitive cells called cones. There are three types of cones; each one detects one color of light—red, green, blue. Staring at one color for a long time can cause cones to stop working for awhile; the other cones then take over and you see a different color from the original—the complementary color.

DP 13: The picture shows a desert; you can tell by the type of plants in the scene. Possible animals: rabbit, snake, insect, lizard, scorpion, desert mouse, desert tortoise.

DP 14: Answers will vary. Food chains should show green plants (producers) and animals (consumers) connected by arrows.

DP 15: Answers will vary. A possible device might repeatedly hurl rocks from various angles.

DP 16: Answers will vary.

DP 17: You'd include information about the equipment, procedure, and results. Scientists need to repeat one another's experiments to verify the results.

DP 18: Galaxies are moving farther apart. The dots on a balloon move apart as the balloon expands.

DP 19: The polar bear covers its nose so that it will blend into the snow without being seen. Possible answers: tiger's stripes help the animal stay hidden while stalking its prey; owls glide silently in the air when looking for food.

DP 20: The ruler does not fall off until more than half of it extends beyond the edge of the table. The ruler, like all objects, has a center of gravity—the point at which it balances (with just as much weight on one side as on the other side). A ruler balances at its center. *Superstar:* If you put an eraser at the end of the ruler that is resting on the table, you can move the other end farther out.

DP 21: Possible reasons: Fossils provide a record of living things and give information about the geologic history of the area.

DP 22: Sounds coming from either side reach one ear before the other; the brain can tell by time difference. Sounds coming from the front or back reach both ears at once.

DP 23: Both sunlight and the light bulb emit light of all colors. Laser light, unlike the light from a flashlight, spreads out very little, making it more powerful. Examples of uses: in surgery; in measuring distances in outer space; in surveying. *Superstar:* Answers will vary.

DP 24: Inclined plane. It is easier to move an object up a slope than to lift it straight up.

DP 25: The sound created with the rubber band around the box is louder. Only a small portion of the air vibrates when the narrow rubber band is plucked. When the box is used, plucking the rubber band also causes the box to vibrate; these vibrations are passed onto the air surrounding the box. Since more air is vibrating, the sound is louder. *Superstar:* The sounds vary because the containers differ in size and their ability to pick up vibrations from the rubber bands.

DP 26: Answers will vary. Students might state obstacles, such as the problem of supplying food for the long trip, or ways to overcome obstacles.

DP 27: Drawings will probably look like blobs. Bones give support. *Superstar:* Animals include jellyfish, worms, insects (exoskeletons), mussels, octopuses, and clams (shells).

DP 28: No sound is made by the hammer. The Moon has no atmosphere, and sound cannot travel through a vacuum. *Superstar:* The astronauts communicated by radio.

DP 29: Answers will vary.

DP 30: Possible answers: cell structure, movement, food-getting, excretion, reproduction, responses; take in oxygen and give off carbon dioxide.

DP 31: The paper lifts upward. When you blow, the air pressure below the paper is greater than above, causing the strip to be pushed upward. The wings of an airplane are designed on this principle. The air flowing over the curved wing moves faster than the air underneath; this makes the air pressure above less than the pressure below. The wing is pushed up into the air.

DP 32: Most scientists classify living things into five kingdoms: monerans, protists, fungi, plants, and animals.

DP 33: The soda stays in the straw because the air pressure pushing up from the bottom of the straw is greater than the pressure at the top. When the finger is removed, the pressures are equal and gravity pulls the soda down.

DP 34: The paper clip moves. Answers will vary depending on the thickness of the materials used. *Superstar:* The number of sheets will vary depending on the strength of the magnet.

DP 35: Drawings will vary. An animal would need to blend in so it could hide from predators or so it could stay hidden when hunting prey.

DP 36: The egg sinks in fresh water and floats in salt water. It's easier to float in the ocean, which is salt water. *Superstar:* Add salt gradually, measuring as you add it.

DP 37: Sea shore or tide pool. The animals mentioned are saltwater shore animals. Other organisms include algae, fish, barnacles, clams, sea weed.

DP 38: Possible answer: Explain that smoking risks include cancer, heart disease, strokes, addiction, teeth stains, harm to others.

DP 39: Students might mention artificial arms, legs, and hands. Modern prosthetics are made of plastic, fiberglass, metal, and wood; some even have electrical components.

DP 40: $1200 \div 300 = 4$ glasses of milk to meet the daily requirement. Calcium is needed for the growth and maintenance of bones and teeth; it also helps blood to clot and muscles to contract. Sources of calcium include dairy products (cheese, yogurt), sardines, and broccoli.

DP 41: A person's genetic makeup is determined by his or her DNA. Since identical twins have the same genetic makeup, their DNA is identical.

DP 42: If a paleontologist finds fossil footprints of a dinosaur and sees that a tail imprint follows, he or she can infer that the dinosaur dragged its tail on the ground. If there are no tail prints, a paleontologist couldn't draw any conclusion about the dinosaur's tail without some other type of supporting evidence.

DP 43: People might think koalas are bears because of their fur, claws, and rounded ears. Differences: reproduction and diet. *Superstar:* Koalas are marsupials; they live in Australia; they are related to the kangaroo and wallaby.

DP 44: Light travels more slowly in water than in air, so the pencil appears to "bend" where air and water meet. The water also magnifies the pencil. *Superstar:* The results are the same.

DP 45: Most water on Earth is salt water. Possible ways to conserve: use low flow toilets, take shorter showers, fix leaks, landscape with plants that need less water.

DP 46: Nerves carry impulses from the retina to the brain. The brain then interprets the image so that is is right side up and the correct size.

DP 47: Answers will vary. *Superstar:* "That's one small step for a man, one giant step for mankind."

DP 48: Possible answers: The adaptation helps other bees pinpoint the location of a food source, so they don't have to search for food. Chimpanzees communicate through vocalizations, facial expressions, posture, touch, and movements.

DP 49: If you hold the bowl of the spoon very close, your reflection is bigger than you; but if you hold it a few inches away, your image is smaller and upside down. In the back of the spoon, your image is smaller and right-side up. The differences are due to the curved surfaces—the bowl curves down in the middle (concave mirror); the back curves up in the middle (convex mirror). A flat mirror gives a more accurate image.

DP 50: Answers should reflect that leaves differ in color, shape, veins, size. *Superstar:*

If conditions change and threaten the survival of plants and animals, differences among species allow some forms to survive.

DP 51: Blood passes from the heart's left side into the aorta (main artery), then into other arteries which lead to capillaries; capillaries join arteries to veins, which take the blood back to the heart's right side; the blood is pumped from the right side of the heart to the lungs, and then it returns to the heart's left side.

DP 52: It's easier to lift the book by pressing on the far end of the ruler—the part that is farthest from the fulcrum. *Superstar:* You can hit the ball farther with a bat: your arm acts as a lever with the fulcrum at the elbow, placing the hitting point farther from the fulcrum; your muscles provide the pushing force.

DP 53: Possible answers: time of sunrise and sunset; air quality index; temperature highs and lows in various cities nationwide and around the world; rainfall for the year; weather forecast.

DP 54: Sound travels better through solids than through air, so they could hear the hoof beats through the ground better than if they were standing and listening for them in the air. Possible demonstration: Have Jill sit at a table and listen while you tap the table. Then have her put her ear to the table while you tap again; the sound should be louder.

DP 55: The surface is covered by pointed and rounded rocks and landforms; drifts that look like dunes; dust and pebbles. Close-up images of the "dunes" indicate that there is sand on Mars' surface. Based on *Pathfinder* pictures and data, scientists think that Mars once had seasonal cycles, clouds, winds, and flowing water.

DP 56: Probable reason is that hummingbirds couldn't fly the great distance across the water. *Superstar:* Red attracts them.

DP 57: Answers will vary. Students should multiply their weights by $\frac{2}{3}$ or 0.67 to find out how much of their bodies is water. Possible answer: Fill a 2-liter bottle with water and weigh it. Divide your weight by the weight of the 2-liter bottle.

DP 58: **A** is the meat-eater (carnivore); its teeth are pointed for biting into and tearing meat. **B** is the plant-eater (herbivore); its teeth are flatter for grinding and mashing plants.

DP 59: Possible answers: object's cellular structure; independent motion; its reaction to environment; its ability to use or make food. A microscope might help. *Superstar:* Answers will vary.

DP 60: Possible answer: There would be no atmosphere; the oceans would float away into space; water wouldn't run downhill; rain wouldn't fall to the ground; the Moon wouldn't stay in orbit around Earth; there would be no tides.

DP 61: When the paper ball is held close to the open eye, it blocks the larger object from view. Diagrams should show the Moon between Earth and Sun, but much closer to the Earth. The Moon's shadow falls on the Sun, blocking it from view. *Superstar:* As the Moon travels around the Earth, its orbit is tilted in relation to the Earth's equator, so the Moon does not often pass directly between the Earth and the Sun.

DP 62: Possible images include car crashes, sickly person, different alcoholic beverages. Possible titles: Alcohol Kills; Is This Really Fun?

DP 63: Possible answers: Arguments for—handy for emergencies; helpful for taking care of business matters; light and easy to carry. Arguments against—a phone limits your enjoyment of nature; a phone may

keep you occupied with work that you're trying to get away from; phones may not work everywhere.

DP 64: Food stuck in the trachea can block the airway and could lead to death. Possible answer: Ask adult for help; call 911; perform the Heimlich maneuver if you know how. *Superstar:* The Heimlich maneuver is a series of forceful pushes between the navel and ribs, designed to force air up the trachea to dislodge the object and force it out of the mouth.

DP 65: Possible answer: Hide the fabric in different environments and see how long it takes people to locate it.

DP 66: Ice hockey—reduce friction by smoothing out the ice so the players can move more easily. Soccer—increase friction by buying new shoes that would give you a better grip on the grass.

DP 67: Owls and falcons hunt and eat such animals as rodents, birds, and rabbits that eat a gardener's crops. The statues are supposed to keep these garden pests away.

DP 68: Fanning with the book speeds up evaporation of the sweat from her skin and brings in cooler air.

DP 69: A comet is a celestial body with a head consisting of a solid nucleus of ice and dust surrounded by a hazy (nebulous) disk (coma) that can be as large as the planet Jupiter; a comet also has a vaporous tail when its orbit passes close to the Sun.

DP 70: Red blood cell. Red blood cells are brighter red when they are oxygen rich; they carry oxygen to all cells and remove carbon dioxide from all cells.

DP 71: Possible answers: Voice gets louder and higher pitched; certain words are emphasized more than others; may sound afraid. Emotion might be shown through differences in rhythm, loudness, inflection, pitch, speed, and enunciation. If a computer's voice sounds emotional people may react and respond to it differently; it also could help a person convey what they are feeling.

DP 72: Answers will vary. Students can look in an encyclopedia or in books about inventors.

DP 73: Water molecules cling together to form a thin surface layer. This property is known as *surface tension*. The soap weakens the water's surface tension at the place where you put your finger and the pepper moves to the edge of the bowl, where the water's surface tension is stronger.

DP 74: Since oxygen is continually being recycled, it's possible that the oxygen in the air today was breathed by dinosaurs.

DP 75: Front—cat, dog, rabbit, parakeet; Back—goldfish, turtle, snake, iguana. Possible answers: warm-blooded (front)—hamsters, mice, rats, other birds; cold-blooded (back)—salamanders, other reptiles and fish.

DP 76: Possible answers: long and short whistles; long and short clicks using two spoons or two sticks. *Superstar:* Answers will vary.

DP 77: Each grain is shaped like a cube. Salt is a crystal because its grains all have the same regular cube shape.

DP 78: One of the dots disappears. The human eye has a "blind spot," a break in the retina where the optic nerve connects to the brain. Images don't form on this spot.

DP 79: Possible answers: toasters, lights, electric ovens, TV, computer, electric heater; light—candles; electric heater—fireplace; electric oven—wood stove.

DP 80: Without sunlight, plants would die. The weather would get cold. The dinosaurs could die from lack of food and warmth.

DP 81: Ribs protect the heart and lungs. Ribs also help control the size of the chest cavity during breathing. When you breathe in, the ribs move up to expand the chest cavity as air is sucked into the lungs; when you breathe out, the ribs move down, allowing the chest cavity to get smaller as air is forced out of the lungs.

DP 82: It is harder to push the air-filled balloon under the water. Air sacs in ducks act like inflated balloons, facilitating floating. Other adaptations: webbed feet, down, bills.

DP 83: Answers will vary.

DP 84: It will be easier for Gretchen to carry the books in a backpack. The backpack will spread the weight out over her whole back; it will also help keep her evenly balanced.

DP 85: Possible answers: With paper and ruler—draw parallel rays falling on the curved surface of Earth to show a greater concentration of direct rays at equator than at the poles. With flashlight and globe, shine flashlight as shown here:

DP 86: Students should see a smiling face. The two pictures move so quickly that the eye sees them as one image. When the pencil is rolled slowly, two separate images are seen. *Superstar:* movies, TV, cartoons.

DP 87: An atom is the smallest part of an element. Its parts are the electrons, protons, and neutrons. *Superstar:* Possible drawing:

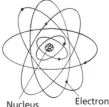

Nucleus (Protons and Neutrons)   Electron

Splitting an atom means splitting the nucleus. This was first done in 1919 by Ernest Rutherford. Splitting at atom releases great amounts of energy and changes one substance into another.

DP 88: Franklin was trying to show that lightning was an electrical charge. Electricity hit the metal rod and passed down the kite string; this could have killed him.

DP 89: The owl and raccoon should be connected by two arrows going in opposite directions.

DP 90: Possible causes: pressure from roots of trees; expansion and contraction of driveway during freezing and thawing; settling of land after the cement was poured; earthquake activity. Answers will vary.

DP 91: Most will feel one pencil point on arm and hands, two on fingertips (closest sensors here).

DP 92: Possible answer: Add a friend to Susan's end; move Ron toward middle. *Superstar:* Balance the ruler on the block. Then add a quarter to one end and a penny to the other. Add more pennies or slide the quarter closer to the fulcrum (block).

DP 93: Steve understands that the area was most likely once underwater. The boys are probably looking at sedimentary rock.

DP 94: Answers will vary. Possible reasons: helps prevent backaches, muscle strains, and neck pains; look taller.

DP 95: Weight changes according to the gravitational pull of a planet, but size doesn't.

DP 96: Answers will vary.

DP 97: A transparent body would make it harder for enemies to see you. Other adaptations: fins, gills, air bladders, streamlined shape.

DP 98: Possible answers: height (children are usually smaller than adults); hair color (older people may have white or gray hair); skin (older people may have wrinkles); type of clothing (some fashions are geared for a certain age group); language (some figures of speech are particular to a specific age group). You can't judge a person's age by looks alone because looks can be deceiving; for example, some adults are shorter than some children. Diet, amount of exercise, body type, heredity, and other factors can also influence how young or old a person looks.

DP 99: Possible questions: Will the chemicals harm humans, pets, or food? Does the liquid freeze plants and other living things besides the termites? Will the chemicals or freezing kill beneficial insects, too?

DP 100: Possible diagram:

He could hold the periscope sideways to see around corners.

DP 101: Sparky will have less time to sleep. Because of the way the Earth is tilted, during the summer Alaska remains in sunlight during most of the day.

DP 102: Using a zigzag motion going up a hill provides a gentler slope, making it easier to go up to a higher level. Similarly, hiking trails zigzag and mountain roads go round and round a mountainside to lessen the slope.

DP 103: Possible arguments: Computers are smarter because they can figure things out faster; they can be programmed to know and apply rules; they can play against humans and win. Computers are not smarter because humans have to program them first; computers can't think for themselves; they can't reason; they can't plug themselves in.

DP 104: Soft body parts such as skin were less likely to become fossils than bones were. The discovery of dinosaur skin impressions gave scientists new information. Scientific models change as new discoveries are made.

DP 105: You could probably hold the pencil for about five minutes. The pencil is light but muscles must support the weight of hand and arm. You could increase strength and endurance by exercising and doing weight training.

DP 106: Possible answers: Age of technology, nuclear power, computers, modern medicine. Reasons should explain how the achievement increased human capabilities.

DP 107: You'd weigh more with wet clothes on because you'd be carrying your own weight plus the weight of the water. Birds don't get heavy and soggy because they have natural oils that keep water from soaking in. Since oil and water don't mix, water rolls off their feathers. Other adaptations: light hollow bones, wings weight.

DP 108: The water evaporated from the ocean; water vapor rose, cooled, and formed clouds; the droplets in the clouds grew and fell to the ground as rain or snow. The rain or snow may fall into the ocean or may run off the land into rivers and flow back to the ocean.

DP 109: Possible answer: Use a paved area and an area with plants; sprinkle equal amounts of water on both areas and see what happens. (The water will quickly run across the paved area.)

DP 110: Answers will vary. Possible answers: wear ear plugs; turn down volume of stereo (especially when wearing headphones); avoid live rock concerts.

DP 111: Answers will vary. Nocturnal animals include raccoons, opossums, owls, skunks, badgers. Students could learn about the animals' hunting habits, night activities, and enemies.

DP 112: The heart pumps blood. Possible questions: Is there life on other planets? What happened to the dinosaurs? How does memory work? Why do we dream?

DP 113: The uncovered finger will feel colder. Animals with blubber include whales, dolphins, seals, and other sea mammals. Blubber helps keep animals warm in cold waters.

DP 114: 1 mile; 2 miles; $\frac{2}{5}$ mile. *Superstar:* Light travels much faster than sound, which travels through air at the rate of about 1,100 feet per second. In 5 seconds, sound travels 5,500 feet (slightly more than a mile).

DP 115: A cat's hair stands on end; the cat looks bigger and more menacing to enemies. People get goose bumps when they are cold or frightened; muscles contract and produce bumps around the hair.

DP 116: If you just let go of the can, you wouldn't have to get out of the way; if no energy is added, the can would swing back to the same place. If you pushed the can away, you'd have to back up; a push adds energy, and the can would swing back farther so that it would hit you if you didn't move away.

DP 117: The inside of the glass gets cloudy because water vapor (moisture) in the warm breath cools and condenses (changes to liquid water) when it hits the cold glass. You see a "cloud" when you blow out a breath on a cold day.

DP 118: You'd see a hole in the hand. Each eye sees a different image, but with both eyes open, the two images are combined in the brain to form one image. This activity works using other objects and different distances.

DP 119: Possible answers: take a break every so often to stretch and rest eyes; put monitor at eye level; support wrists; use correct desk height.

DP 120: Possible answer: the discovery of penicillin. Answers will vary.

DP 121: Procedures and predictions will vary. Student plans should include controlling all variables except dark and light; then controlling all variables except for temperature. *Superstar:* Seeds will sprout better in warmth; seeds will sprout both in the light and in the dark.

DP 122: Possible answer: Enclose a bowl of sea water in the plastic bag. In the sun, the water will evaporate and leave the salt behind. When the air inside the bag becomes saturated with water vapor, the fresh water will condense on the sides and bottom of the bag. Ocean water is too salty to drink. *Superstar:* Results will vary depending on student designs.

DP 123: Anna is right. Reasons: seals are warm-blooded; they bear live young; they nurse their young; they have lungs, not gills, for breathing.

DP 124: Use the magnet to maneuver the nail to the side of the glass, then up along the side until it is out of the water. A magnet works through glass; it will attract the nail but not the plastic button.

DP 125: An igneous rock. Possible answers: it's hard; takes heat; is beautiful. Other uses: floors, patios, monuments, stone walls, fireplaces.

DP 126: Caution Ali not to eat them. Eating wild mushrooms can cause death. Even those that look like supermarket mushrooms can be poisonous. *Superstar:* Mushrooms are fungi. They are decomposers, helping to break down decaying matter into small pieces that will eventually form new soil.

DP 127: Possible reasons include concern for the fish, pollution of beaches downstream, contamination of freshwater supply.

DP 128: The Achilles tendon connects the muscle in the calf to the heel and contracts to move the foot. If it is cut or torn, you can't walk or run.

DP 129: The right hand feels cooler. The water evaporates. Evaporation has a cooling effect because it takes heat energy away from the skin. *Superstar:* Perspiration helps cool down the body when you're hot.

DP 130: Answers will vary.

DP 131: The pointed end of the crayon sinks deeper into the clay than the flat end. Broad hooves help keep the caribou from sinking in snow.

DP 132: Place the ruler on the desk so that one end of the ruler sticks out beyond the edge. Put an eraser or a paper clip on the other end of the ruler. Press down on the opposite end of the ruler to lift the eraser or paper clip in the air. *Superstar:* The fulcrum is the edge of the desk. The load is the eraser or paper clip.

DP 133: The water swirls and a vortex is created. A vortex is a mass of liquid that has a cavity in the center. The vortex deepens and the water rises around the sides as it swirls faster. Tornadoes and whirlpools swirl like the liquid in the container.

DP 134: Too much exposure to sunlight damages delicate skin tissues and causes changes that may lead to cancer. Bright sunlight can also damage eyes. Possible protection: wear sunscreen; avoid outdoor activities between 10:00 a.m. and 3:00 p.m.; wear protective clothes (long sleeves, hat, sunglasses); use an umbrella to shield you from the sun.

DP 135: Possible answers: Add layers of clothes (insulation); rub hands together (friction produces heat); light a fire (chemical reaction produces heat); stand near a light bulb (light generates heat); use electric heater (electricity produces heat); exercise (metabolic activity releases heat). Possible inventions: heaters, electric blankets, heat lamps, treadmills and other exercise equipment.

DP 136: Possible answers: diamond—hard, transparent, shiny; graphite—black, soft, smooth. The arrangement of the atoms (in crystal structures) account for the differences in diamond and graphite.

DP 137: Possible answers: Stroke the needle about 20 times with the magnet, then use the needle to pick up a paper clip. Hang a paper clip from the magnet, then hang another paper clip from the first paper clip. *Superstar:* Plans and results will vary.

DP 138: Mary is right. The light bulb will light in **A**, but not in **B** because nails conduct electricity; wood does not.

DP 139: Possible answer: Try to guide the butterfly out the door or an open window.

DP 140: Possible answers: levers—nutcracker, pliers, hammer; wedge—chisel, knife; screw—screws, bolts; inclined plane—ramp, dustpan; pulley—drapery rods, crane; wheel and axle—eggbeater, bike.

DP 141: Because the Earth rotates from east to west, the prevailing winds in the

Northern Hemisphere blow from west to east. When the plane travels with the wind, the trip is shorter; when it travels against the wind, it takes longer.

DP 142: Answers will vary. Erwin is probably right. The mother may be foraging nearby for food. If there is a human smell on the fawn, the mother may abandon it. The boys could call a zoo or an animal rescue shelter for more information.

DP 143: You would have to be more careful with the pan with the metal handle; metal gets hotter because it's a better conductor of heat than rubber.

DP 144: Possible answers: diphtheria, whooping cough, tetanus, mumps, measles, polio. *Superstar:* Edward Jenner developed a vaccination against smallpox. Students could look in an encyclopedia or in a book about disease prevention.

WEEKLY PUZZLERS

WP 1: If an animal is a vertebrate, you know it has a backbone. The five main classes of vertebrates are: fish, amphibians, reptiles, birds, and mammals.

WP 2: red + yellow = orange; red + blue = purple; blue + yellow = green; red + yellow + blue = dark brown to black; Answers will vary; students will find that reversing positions makes no difference but that intensifying colors may make a difference.

WP 3: Answers will vary, but mold will grow on all the materials, showing signs of decay.

WP 4: Procedures and results will vary. Students may use such materials as cloth, paper, aluminum foil, or wire mesh in varying thicknesses. They should place these between the magnet and an object that the magnet will pick up, such as a nail or paper clip. Stronger magnets will attract objects through thicker layers of materials.

WP 5: Answers will vary.

WP 6: Most students will find that they shrink during the day. The cartilage disks between the vertebrae of the spinal column compress during the day. During sleep, the full height is restored. *Superstar:* Answers will vary.

WP 7: Answers will vary. There are temperature ranges because the Earth is heated by the Sun during the day, but cools off at night. Other factors include distance from the equator—places farther north generally have cooler temperatures than those farther south; the influence of oceans—places near the ocean usually have milder temperatures than places inland; altitude—places higher in altitude often have cooler temperatures. *Superstar:* Answers will vary, but should reflect the information presented in students' graphs.

WP 8: 1961—first human space flights; 1965—first space walks; 1969—first human lands on the Moon; 1986—Challenger explodes; 1990—Hubble telescope launched into space; 1997—*Pathfinder* lands on Mars. The space-related events in each student's lifetime will vary.

WP 9: The newspaper changes color everywhere except where it was shielded from the light by the objects on top of it. Fading is a chemical change. (Paper has dyes in it that change chemically in sunlight.) Chemical changes are permanent; physical changes are usually reversible. *Superstar:* Possible answers: Burning the paper is a chemical change. Folding, tearing, or cutting the paper is a physical change.

WP 10: The water carves a path through the soil. As the water flows, it takes away some of the soil and deposits it at the bottom of

the cardboard. Rivers wear away land by carrying away soil and bits of rock.

WP 11: You couldn't breathe. The leaves treated with petroleum jelly turn yellow and start to wither. The untreated leaves remain green. Carbon dioxide, a raw material necessary for photosynthesis, cannot enter the treated leaves because the pores through which gases enter and leave are blocked. Since photosynthesis cannot take place, the leaves die. *Superstar:* carbon dioxide.

WP 12: Answers will vary. Students will probably conclude that it takes more effort to do the tasks and that civilization would not have the art, architecture, or sculpture it has. Also, many mechanical devices would be quite different.

WP 13: The flashlight represents the Sun. When the light shines directly on the glass, there is a blue tinge. When the light shines from an angle, there is a pink or orange tinge. During the day, when the Sun hits the atmosphere more directly, the gases in the air reflect mostly blue light from the Sun. At sunrise and sunset, when the Sun is lower in the sky, more red light is reflected.

WP 14: The circumference of the balloon decreases after the balloon has been in the freezer for a couple of hours. Air contracts as it gets colder. *Superstar:* The circumference of a balloon filled with water increases after the balloon has been in the freezer for a couple of hours. As water freezes, it expands—an important exception to the general rule that most materials contract when cooled.

WP 15: Answers will vary. One possible method is to produce signs that are identical except for color. Ask helpers to walk toward the signs and say when they can read each one. *Superstar:* Method can be similar but should be carried out at night.

WP 16: Possible answers: 1. Rain forests are found in the tropics. 2. They are habitat for many plants and animals; prevent global warming; are home to native peoples; are called the "lungs" of the earth because of the oxygen given off by rain forest trees and plants. 3. They're endangered because their trees are cut down for timber, agricultural land, and ranching. 4. These forests are warm and wet all year. Rain forests may receive 300 inches of rainfall a year. There are more species of plants and animals in rain forests than in all other ecosystems of the world combined.

WP 17: Procedures will vary. Students could set up two lights—one bright, one less bright—at the same distance from a specific point and ask helpers to guess which is closer. A weaker source of light will look farther away than a bright source, even if they are the same distance away. When you look at the stars in the sky, you might think the brighter stars are closer to the Earth, but that's not necessarily true.

WP 18: Turn over the bottle so that the opening is at the bottom. (Cap it or hold your thumb over the opening so that the liquids don't spill out.) The oil will still float on the water, but the water will be near the opening. Tip the bottle slightly, remove the cover or your thumb, and pour off the water.

WP 19: Half the celery turns red and the other half turns blue. The water moved up the stem through thin tubes in the celery stalks. You can see the ends of these tubes when you look at the bottom of the stalk. The water is kept separate as it moves up the stem.

WP 20: The ice cube covered with dirt will melt faster than the uncovered cube because dark colors absorb solar energy (sunlight) better than light colors. You use

identical variables to be sure your results are due to the dirt, not the size of the ice cube. Light clothing wouldn't get as hot as dark clothing.

WP 21: Possible ideas: get bones from a roast chicken and try to assemble parts of the skeleton; cut puzzle pieces from cardboard or paper and have a person try putting the pieces together. Give the person only three of the pieces and see if it's harder to reconstruct the fossil.

WP 22: Some of the water in the jar gets replaced by air. Measure how much water is replaced by air. The air in the jar comes from the lungs. The measure of lung capacity is imprecise because some water may be lost as the jar is inverted; also, some of the air from the lungs may bubble up to the surface outside the jar opening.

WP 23: Wearing many thin layers keeps you warmer than wearing one thick one. Air trapped between the many layers acts as insulation, keeping the body's heat from escaping into the surrounding cold air. Possible procedure: Wrap one thermometer in a very thick garment or cloth, another in many thin layers of cloth. Put both in the refrigerator. Check the temperatures after an hour.

WP 24: Answers will vary.

WP 25: Answers will vary.

WP 26: The balloon starts to inflate. A chemical reaction between the vinegar and the baking soda produces a gas—carbon dioxide; when carbon dioxide is added to the air in the bottle, it increases the total volume of gas and expands the balloon more.

WP 27: 1.–4. Answers will vary; 5. pollen grains; 6. the pistil may not have all the parts in the drawing; seeds may be absent or very small.

WP 28: The balloon will become positively or negatively charged, depending on the fabric on which it was rubbed. Either charge will attract small pieces of paper, eraser rubbings, hair, and will attract a stream of water.

WP 29: Answers will vary. Scientists know the relative dates of appearance of these life forms on Earth through fossil evidence. The timeline indicates that people have been around only a short time relative to the history of life on Earth.

WP 30: Answers will vary.

WP 31: Since everyone's fingerprints are different, they can be used to identify each individual. The three basic kinds of fingerprints are whorl, arch, and loop.

WP 32: The coastlines have a rough fit. These continents were once part of one large continent that broke apart; the continents are still spreading apart. *Superstar:* Answers will vary.

WP 33: Answers will vary. *Superstar:* Answers will vary.

WP 34: Models will vary. The model can be altered by making a vertical cross-section of the first model. Plastic, glass, or transparent wrap can be used to seal the cut edge of the cross-section.

WP 35: Answers will vary. Students should be able to get closer without shoes on than with the pennies taped to the bottom of their shoes. Retractable claws and fur pads help the tiger silently approach its prey.

WP 36: When the notches are lined up, the light from the flashlight shines through to the unnotched card. When the notches don't line up, the light does not reach the unnotched card. Light travels in a straight line.